**Come up and
see me sometime**

Come up and
see me sometime

BROWN
DOG
BOOKS

Classic Pick Ups

What do you advise for a man who's both hungry and lonesome and who hates to eat alone?

**Pat Denning (George Brent)
to Peggy Sawyer (Ruby Keeler)**
42nd Street, 1933

Your hair is like a field of silver daisies. I'd like to run barefoot through your hair!

**Gifford Middleton (Franchot Tone)
to Lola Burns (Jean Harlow)**
Bombshell, 1933

Was that cannon fire, or is it my heart pounding?

**Ilsa Lund Laszlo (Ingrid Bergman)
to Rick Blain (Humphrey Bogart)**
Casablanca, 1942

Oh, Miss Pipperidge, I'm just crazy fer you! Why, just to see your lovely smile I'd swim through beer with my mouth closed!

Jigger Craigin (Cameron Mitchell) to Carrie Pipperidge (Barbara Ruick)
Carousel, **1956**

If you aren't decent, boyfriend, you'll do until something decent comes along.

Dolly Portland (Jean Harlow) to Captain Alan Gaskell (Clark Gable)
China Seas, **1935**

You're not very
bright, are you?
I like that in a man.

**Matty Walker (Kathleen Turner)
to Ned Racine (William Hurt)
Body Heat, 1981**

Mind if I get drunk with you?

Vantine Jefferson (Jean Harlow) to Dennis Carson (Clark Gable)
Red Dust, 1932

Mae West
American actress (1893–1980)

Is that a gun in your pocket or are you just glad to see me?

Peel Me a Grape, 1975

Why don't you come up and see me sometime . . . when I've got nothin' on but the radio.

I'm No Angel, 1933

Mae: How tall are you?
Man: Six foot seven.
Mae: Let's forget the six feet and talk about the seven inches.

Quoted in G Eells and S Musgrove's biography *Mae West,* 1989

Let's get out of these wet
clothes and into a dry martini.

Every Day's a Holiday, 1937

We're going to know each other eventually, why not now?

Rick Leland (Humphrey Bogart) to Alberta Marlow (Mary Astor)
Across the Pacific, 1942

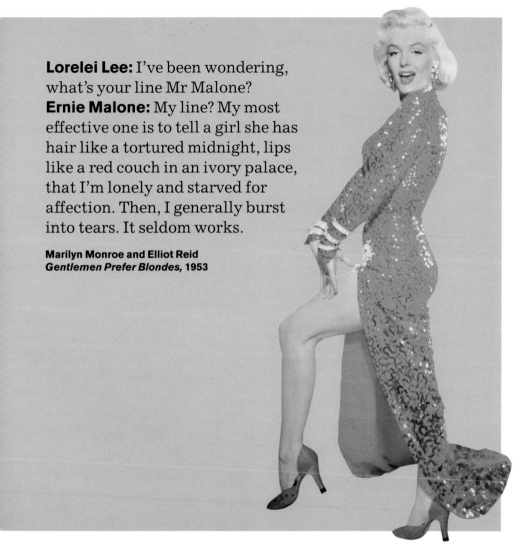

Lorelei Lee: I've been wondering, what's your line Mr Malone?
Ernie Malone: My line? My most effective one is to tell a girl she has hair like a tortured midnight, lips like a red couch in an ivory palace, that I'm lonely and starved for affection. Then, I generally burst into tears. It seldom works.

Marilyn Monroe and Elliot Reid
Gentlemen Prefer Blondes, 1953

Give me a kiss
or I'll sock you.

**Frank Chambers (John Garfield)
to Cora Smith (Lana Turner)
*The Postman Always Rings
Twice*, 1946**

Matthew Hollis:
Kiss you? I ought to spank you!
Jennifer Lyons:
Oh, please, and bite me too.

**Michael Caine and Michelle Johnson
Blame it on Rio, 1984**

Wanna dance or
would you rather
just suck face?

**Norman Thayer Jr. (Henry Fonda) to
Ethel Thayer (Katherine Hepburn)
On Golden Pond, 1981**

James Bond:

I admire your courage, Miss . . .?

Sylvia Trench:

Trench. Sylvia Trench.
I admire your luck, Mr . . .?

James Bond:

Bond. James Bond.

Sean Connery and Eunice Gayson
Dr. No, 1962

Tell me about yourself—
your struggles, your
dreams, your telephone
number.

**Peter Arno, American cartoonist
(1904-1968)**

You're a swell dish. I think
I'm gonna go for you.

**Tom Powers (James Cagney)
to Gwen Allen (Jean Harlow)
The Public Enemy, 1931**

Won't you come into the
garden? I would like my
roses to see you.

**Richard Brinsley Sheridan,
English dramatist and politician
(1751-1816).**

What's the matter with me? I'm gay, I'm loveable, and I've got good teeth.

**Carey Jackson (Robert Montgomery)
to Linda Gilman (Bette Davis)
June Bride, 1948.**

Swoon. I'll catch you.

**Almásy (Ralph Fiennes)
to Katharine Clifton (Kristen Scott Thomas)
The English Patient, 1996**

Woody Allen

American actor, author, screenwriter, and film director (1935–)

I had a mad impulse to throw you down on the lunar surface and commit interstellar perversion.

Isaac Davis
Manhattan, 1979

Is sex dirty? Only if it's done right.

Everything You Always Wanted to Know About Sex * But Were Afraid to Ask, 1972

Allan Felix: What are you planning on doing Saturday night?
Museum girl: Committing suicide!
Allan Felix: Well how about Friday night?

Woody Allen to Diane Davila
Play it Again, Sam, 1972

Countess Alexandrovna:
My bedroom at midnight?

Boris:
Perfect. Will you be there too?

Olga Georges-Picot and Woody Allen
Love and Death, 1975

Peter Joshua: Do we know each other?
Regina Lampert: Why, do you think we're going to? Because I already know an awful lot of people and until one of them dies I couldn't possibly meet anyone else.
Peter Joshua: Well, if anyone goes on the critical list, let me know.

Cary Grant and Audrey Hepburn
Charade, 1963

Let's go somewhere we can be alone. Ah, there doesn't seem to be anyone on this couch.

S Quentin Quale (Groucho Marx) seducing a love interest
Go West, 1940

You're beautiful when you're angry.

Colonel Pieter Deventer (Clark Gable) to Carla Van Oven (Lana Turner)
Betrayed, 1954

Your eyes are amazing do you know that?
You should never shut them, not even at night.

**Paul Martel (Oliver Martinez)
to Connie Sumner (Dianne Lane)**
Unfaithful, 2002

Everything wrong
with you I like.

**Captain Randall (Van Johnson)
to Dorinda Durston (Irene Dunne)**
A Guy Named Joe, 1944

Gwen Allen: I'm not accustomed to riding with strangers.
Tom Powers: We're not gonna be strangers.

Jean Harlow and James Cagney
The Public Enemy, 1931

Hi, I'm Mr Right. Someone said you were looking for me?

(Lick finger and wipe on her shirt) . . .
Let's get you out of these wet clothes.

Can I buy you a drink or do you just want the money?

I'd really like to see how you look when I'm naked.

Do you believe in love at first sight or should I walk by again?

Mike Myers as *Austin Powers*

Jerry Mulligan: That's quite a dress you almost have on.
Milo Roberts: Thanks.
Jerry Mulligan: What holds it up?
Milo Roberts: Modesty.

Gene Kelly and Nina Foch
An American in Paris, **1951**

I'll come and make love to you at five o'clock. If I'm late, start without me.

Tallulah Bankhead, American actress (1903–1968)

Perfect Put Downs

You know something, Hank? You're 90% man and 10% rat!

Kit Jordon (Lana Turner) to Hank Walker (Hugh O'Brien)
Love Has Many Faces, 1965

Woman: How do you write women so well?
Melvin Udall: I think of a man, and I take away reason and accountability.

Melvin Udall (Jack Nicholson) to woman (Julie Benz)
As Good As It Gets, 1997

Great. A woman friend. You know you may be the first attractive woman I have not wanted to sleep with in my entire life.

Harry Burns (Billy Crystal) to Sally Albright (Meg Ryan)
When Harry Met Sally, **1989**

I've had a perfectly wonderful evening.
But this wasn't it.

Do you think I could buy back my
introduction to you?

I never forget a face, but in your case I'll be glad to make an exception.

Women should be obscene
and not heard.

She got her looks from her father.
He's a plastic surgeon.

Groucho Marx, American actor (1890–1977)

Terry McKay: It's not that I'm prudish, but my mother told me never to enter a man's room in months ending in "R."
Nickie Ferrante: Well, your mother's not only smart, she's pretty too.
Terry McKay: Tell me, have you been getting results with a line like that, or would I be surprised?
Nickie Ferrante: If you'd be surprised, I'd be surprised.

Deborah Kerr and Cary Grant
An Affair to Remember, **1957**

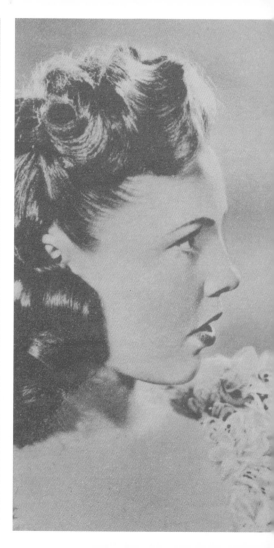

I have a previous
engagement, which
I will make as soon
as possible.

**John Barrymore, American actor
(1882–1942)**

I've met a lot of hard-
boiled eggs in my time,
but you – you're twenty
minutes.

**Lorraine Minosa (Jan Sterling) to
Chuck Tatum (Kirk Douglas)
Ace in the Hole, 1951**

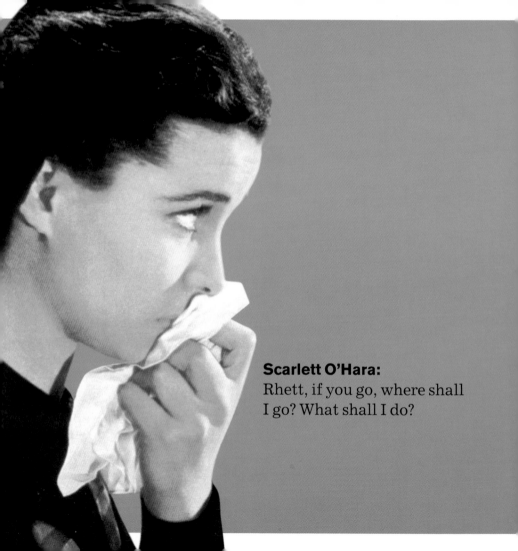

Scarlett O'Hara:

Rhett, if you go, where shall I go? What shall I do?

Rhett Butler:
Frankly, my dear,
I don't give a damn

Vivien Leigh and Clark Gable
Gone with the Wind, 1939

Mr. Allen, this may come as a shock to you, but there are some men who don't end every sentence with a proposition.

Jan Morrow (Doris Day) to Brad Allen (Rock Hudson)
Pillow Talk, 1959

Philip Marlowe: Did I hurt you much, sugar? **Agnes Lowzier:** You and every other man I've ever met.

Sonia Darrin and Humphrey Bogart
The Big Sleep, 1946

Your idea of fidelity is not having more than one man in the bed at the same time.

**Dick Bogarde (Robert Gold)
to Julie Christie (Diana Scott)
Darling, 1965**

Dorothy Parker
American writer (1893–1967)

Wit has truth in it; wisecracking is simply calisthenics with words.

She (Dame Edith Evans) looks like something that would eat its young.

The first thing I do in the morning is brush my teeth and sharpen my tongue.

She (Katherine Hepburn) runs the gamut of emotions from A to B.

Beauty is only skin deep, but ugly goes clean to the bone.

Claude Horton: So, my haughty lady . . . I'm not good enough for you, eh?
Nettie Horton: Well, it finally dawned on you.
Claude Horton: So you admit that you've been carrying on with the butler!
Nettie: Which butler?

Robert Woolsey and Patricia Wilder
On Again Off Again, 1937

Garrett Breedlove:
I like the lights on.
Aurora Greenway:
Then go home and
turn them on.

Jack Nicholson and Shirley MacLaine
Terms of Endearment, 1983

Bud Baxter: Did you hear what I said, Miss Kubelik? I absolutely adore you.
Fran Kubelik: Shut up and deal.

Jack Lemmon and Shirley Maclaine
The Apartment, 1960

Winston Churchill

(1874–1965)
British Prime Minister
1940–1945, 1951–1955

Lady Nancy Astor:
Winston, if you were my husband I should flavour your coffee with poison.
Churchill: Madam, if I were your husband, I should drink it.

Bessie Braddock:
Winston, you're drunk.
Churchill: Bessie, you're ugly. But tomorrow I shall be sober.

Anonymous Member of Parliament to Churchill:
Must you fall asleep when I'm speaking?
Churchill: No, it's purely voluntary.

Anonymous woman to Churchill:
There are two things I don't like about you, Mr. Churchill—your politics and your moustache.
Churchill: My dear madam, pray do not disturb yourself. You are not likely to come into contact with either.

When I first saw you,
I thought you were handsome.
Then, of course, you spoke.

Carol Connelly (Helen Hunt) to Melvin Udall (Jack Nicholson)
As Good As It Gets, 1997

Addison DeWitt:
What do you take me for?
Eve Harrington:
I don't know that I'd take you for anything.

Anne Baxter to George Sanders
All About Eve, 1950

Librarian: You know, you don't look like a man
who'd be interested in first editions.
Phillip Marlowe: I collect blondes and bottles too.

Carole Douglas and Humphrey Bogart
The Big Sleep, 1946

If you were more of a woman, I would be more of a man. Kissing you is like kissing the side of a beer bottle.

Laurence Harvey to his costar Capucine during the filming of *A Walk on the Wild Side*, 1962

I'd love to kiss you, but I just washed my hair.

Madge Norwood (Bette Davis) to Marvin Blake (Richard Barthelmess) *Cabin in the Cotton*, 1932

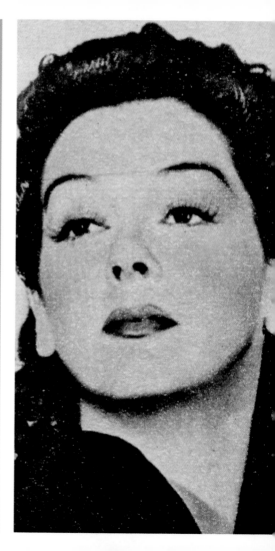

Normally, someone would have to go to a bowling alley to meet someone of your stature.

Hobson (John Gielgud) to Linda Marolla (Liza Minelli) *Arthur*, 1981

I wouldn't go on living with you if you were dipped in platinum.

Lucy Warriner (Irene Dunne) to Jerry Warriner (Cary Grant) *The Awful Truth*, 1937

Oscar Wilde:
Mind if I smoke?

Sarah Bernhardt:
I don't care if
you burn.

Oscar Wilde, Irish dramatist
(1854-1900) and Sarah Bernhardt,
French actress, (1844–1923)

First Published in 2006 in the United Kingdom by

Brown Dog Books
6 The Old Dairy
Melcombe Road
Bath
BA2 3LR

Brown Dog Books is an imprint of The Manning Partnership.
www.manning-partnership.co.uk

Copyright © Elwin Street Limited 2005

Conceived and produced by
Elwin Street Limited
79 St John St
London EC1M 4NR
www.elwinstreet.com

10-digit ISBN 1-90-305620-9
13-digit ISBN 978-1-903056-20-2

Picture credits
Rex Features: Front cover; pages 4, 11,12, 18, 24, 30, 38, 42, 44, 48, 52, 54, 56, 62
Getty Images: page 15

Designed by Rod Teasdale
Printed in China
10 9 8 7 6 5 4 3 2 1